# This book belongs to...

_____

# ALFIE & MILO
## and the
## the CHRISTMAS RESCUE

### Stories by
# Nana Dee

DEDICATED TO
all the little ones
who love adventure,
may you always follow your
curiosity and imagination.
With warm wishes,
*Nana Dee*

© 2025 Nana Dee. All rights reserved.
No part of this publication may be reproduced, stored in a retrieval system, or transmitted in any form or by any means—electronic, mechanical, photocopying, recording, or otherwise—without the prior written permission of the copyright owner.

With warm wishes, Nana Dee

ISBN 978-1-0681701-3-3
Printed in the United Kingdom

Alfie and Milo watched the snow fall, wondering what magic the night would bring.

But then, Alfie and Milo noticed someting moving in the snowy yard...

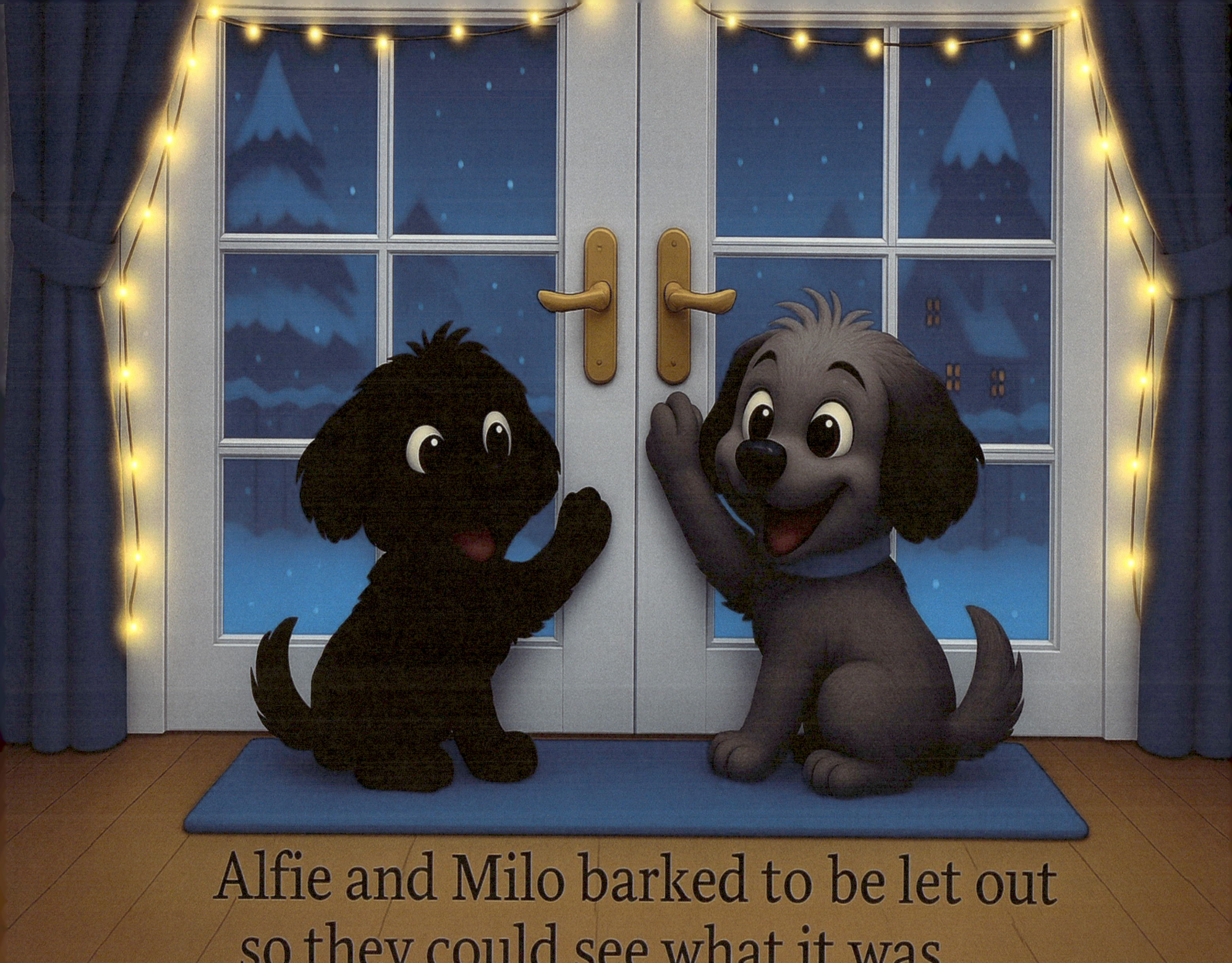

Alfie and Milo barked to be let out so they could see what it was.

At last, the doors opened, Alfie and Milo bounded into the snowy garden.

In the snow, Alfie and Milo found a pille of lost toys. Perhaps these belonged to children nearby, or maybe Santa had dropped them! The pups knew they had to help return them.

An elf appeared from across the garden. 'Hello,' he said, 'can you help me?'"

The little elf sighed, "I'm lost... and I can't find my way back to Santa."

"Santa's sleigh isn't far," the elf sighed. "But without my magic, I can't get there."

Alfie and Milo wagged their tails.
"We will help you find Santa!"

Together, they set off into the snowy night.

The elf pointed to he snowy ground. 'Look—reindeer tracks!" Alfie and Milo leaned closer, there

They hurried along the reindeer tracks—
Santa must be near!

In the street, Alfie and Milo spotted something glimmer in the snow, As they leaned closer, their tails wagging, they saw it was a bell from Santa's sleigh!

The elf shook the bell with all his might. A burst of golden light shot into the sky, calling Santa closer.

The golden light flickered, then dimmed until only tiny sparks remained. Alfie and Milo's ears drooped— what if Santa couldn't see them now?

Alfie offered a reassuring smile. "Don't worry," he said. "We'll look for more clues."

Together, they walked further down the snowy street, searching for more clues.

Eventually, they came across a field and found Comet, one of Santa's reindeer.

Comet told them, "Santa is stuck in the snow!"

With urgency, Comet led them through the snow to help Santa.

Suddenly, the wind howled and the snow began to swirl. The path ahead was hard to see, but Comet urged them on. "Stay close, we'll make it through together!"

Through the blizzard, a faint golden light glimmered ahea
Hope sparked in their hearts—they weren't far now.

At last, they found Santa's sleigh—tipped on its side and buried in snow. Santa needed their help.

Together, they began to dig and pull, determined to set Santa free

At last, Santa and his sleigh were free. He brushed off the snow and smiled at his friends.

"Thank you, Alfie and Milo," said Santa kindly. You've saved Christmas!

Santa chuckled softly, "You've both been such a big help tonight," he said. "How would you like to come with me to help deliver the presents? But first, we must get to the North Pole for more toys!' Alfie wagged his tail,

Up, up they went! Comet lifted the sleigh high above the snowy hills. Alfie and Milo peeked over the side, their tails wagging as the stars twinkled all around them.

Santa smiled down at Alfie and Milo, his eyes twinkling. "*You know,*" he said thoughtfully, "I could really use a little extra help tonight..." The pups began to bounce with excitement, tails wagging faster than ever.

The sleigh glided to a stop outside Santa's workshop. Lights twinkled and smoke curled from the chimneys. Alfie and Milo wagged their tails, gazing at the magical North Pole for the very first time.

Santa smiled as he showed Alfie and Milo around the workshop, "This," he said proudly, "is where Christmas dreams come to life!"

"Time to get the rest of the toys ready to deliver!" said Santa cheerfully. Alfie and Milo jumped up and down with elves hurried to load the sleigh with sparkling giifts.

"We'd better get ready to go." said Santa with a smile. Alfie and Milo barked happily, their tails wagging as the ellves

Up, up they went! The sleigh soared into the starry sky, pulled by Comet's mighty hooves, Alfie and Milo's tails wagged with joy as they flew past the glowing Northern Lights.

The sleigh touched down softly on a snowy rooftop. "Time to deliver some presents!" whispered Santa. Alfie and Milo's eyes sparkled with excitement as they peered over the edge, their tails wagging in

Santa lifted his hand and a swirl of golden sparkles danced through the a
"This is how the presents reach every home," he whispered with a wink.
Alfie and Milo watched in amazement as the magic twinkled toward chim

Santa and the pups flew from house to house, delivering gifts through the starry night. At last, Santa smiled. "Now it's time to take Alfie and Milo home."

The sleigh landed softly outside the gate. Home at last, thought Santa with a smile. Alfie and Milo wagged their tails, ready to snuggle up by the fire.

Santa bent down and gave Alfie and Milo a gentle pat. 'You've been wonderful helpers,' he said kindly. 'Merry Christmas, my brave little friends.'

Alfie and Milo ran through the snow toward their warm, cozy home. Inside, the fire crackled and twinkling lights glowed. It had been a magical Christmas adventure.

Alfie and Milo curled up by the fire as Santa flew past the window. Soon, they drifted off to sleep, dreaming of their next adventure.

High above the sleepy town, Santa smiled and called out, 'Merry Christmas, everyone!" His voice echoed through the night as Comet soared into the stars. Then he turned with a twinkle in his eye and said, 'Merry Christmas to you too!"

# ABOUT THE AUTHOR

Nana Dee has a big heart for storytelling and imagination. Inspired by her family and her love for animals, she brings Alfie and Milo's adventures to life with warmth. She hopes her stories spark joy, courage, and magical dreams in every child who reads them.

www.ingramcontent.com/pod-product-compliance
Lightning Source LLC
Chambersburg PA
CBHW040300100526
44584CB00004BA/292